BRITAIN IN OLD PHOTOGRAPHS

SWINDON

A Fifth Selection

THE SWINDON SOCIETY

SALUBRITAS · ET · INDUSTRIA

ALAN SUTTON PUBLISHING LIMITED

Alan Sutton Publishing Limited
Phoenix Mill · Far Thrupp · Stroud
Gloucestershire · GL5 2BU

First published 1995

Cover photographs: (front) Town Hall, decorated for the Coronation of King George V and Queen Mary, June 1911; (back) Drake Bros, Tennyson Street, 1908.

British Library Cataloguing in Publication Data.
A catalogue record for this book is available from the British Library.

ISBN 0-7509-1032-1

Typeset in 9/10 Sabon.
Typesetting and origination by
Alan Sutton Publishing Limited.
Printed in Great Britain by
Ebenezer Baylis, Worcester.

An early view of the Town Hall at Regent Circus, *c.* 1920. Note the ornate water fountain in the centre of the picture.

Contents

	Introduction	5
1.	Memories of Old Town	7
2.	The Railway Town	27
3.	Streets & Shops	39
4.	Industries & Local Business	53
5.	Rodbourne & Moredon	75
6.	Community Life in Swindon	83
7.	Events & Celebrations	97
8.	Sport & Entertainment	107
9.	Through the Lens of Albert Beaney	123
10.	War to Victory	133
11.	The Changing Face of Swindon	145
	Acknowledgements	158

Les and Derrick ('Dutchy') Hawkins outside their home at 91 Redcliffe Street, Rodbourne, *c.* 1930.

View looking west down Kingshill Road from the junction with Bath Road, *c.* 1895. Named after the King family, local landowners and farmers. The houses on the right were built by Thomas Turner of Drove Road, his 'old man's face' decorated keystone can still be seen today above the windows and doorways.

Introduction

Since the publication of the fourth selection of *Swindon in Old Photographs* in 1993 there have been many requests for yet another glimpse into the past of our town. Once again the Society has attempted to bring the past back to life in this new collection of photographs of Swindon in former years. The people of the town over the years are here pictured at work and play, including scenes showing the diverse social and cultural life of Swindon. Many views of local industries and family businesses, some now gone, but all remembered, are included within these pages. In the year that we commemorate the end of the Second World War, the celebrations in the town are shown, together with some views of life in Swindon during those long years of war and shortages.

Among the photographs included are scenes showing the famous tram crash of 1906, the disastrous fire at Garrards factory in 1958, visits by royalty and the originator of the Scout movement, Baden-Powell, vintage photographs of Swindon's own fun-fair proprietor, Edwards, traction engines at work in Barnes' sawmills at Rushey Platt, the famous Swindon GWR Male Voice Choir, the Marlborough–Swindon Camp Club, and some views taken inside the Great Western Railway Works.

The work of local photographer Albert Beaney is highlighted, showing a selection of his evocative pictures taken around the town between 1935 and 1955. A lifelong resident of Swindon, Albert (now 82 years old) took his first photograph in about 1925, probably with a Brownie camera. In 1937 he lost his job in the Railway Works so he took to the streets with his camera and soon won the trust of the children, catching them at play and unaware of his presence; sometimes they would pose for him in small groups. When he lived in Beatrice Street he displayed his work in the front window for all to see and found ready sales at the homes of his subjects, for what parent could resist the happy faces of the children at play!

Beaney's name will be added to the long list of local Swindon photographers whom we have to thank for recording the events and day to day life in the town. Those names range from the likes of Zephaniah Dodson in the 1870s through the Protheroes, George and Ada Stone, Henry Hemmins, Jules Guggenheim, J. Clarence Hood, Simons, and possibly the most famous of them all, William Hooper, then later Arthur Banbury, Fred Palmer, Leonard C. Maylott, Beatrice Bollard, and more recently, the Society's own Denis Bird.

It is hoped that this latest collection of photographs, the vast majority of which have not been published before, will again bring back memories to old Swindonians and perhaps enable newcomers to the area to learn more of the heritage and past of our town.

Section One

MEMORIES OF OLD TOWN

Corn Exchange and the Rink cinema, Market Square, c. 1925. The Rink cinema is showing a cowboy film, Riders of the Dark, *starring Tim McCoy. Note the overhead power cables for the tramcars; the Old Town terminus was at the Square. To the left is the Corn Exchange, which opened in 1886, with the Old Town Hall building, built in 1852, to the right. Brown & Plummers, wine merchants, occupied both the ground floor of the Town Hall and the building to the right, now demolished. (See also* Swindon in Old Photographs I, *pp. 20 and 114.)*

High Street, Old Town, *c.* 1923. To the left can be seen the canopy over the Bell Hotel, which has since been removed.

The North Wilts Motor Cycle Club reliability trial, 25 March 1921. This was taken by the local photographer Colville. On the left is the old stone building used by Skurrays Garage before their mock-Tudor showrooms were built in 1927. (See *Swindon in Old Photographs I*, pp. 95–6).

High Street, looking north-east, January 1965. Masons grocery shop stood on the corner of the Market Square for many years. In the distance can be seen the entrance to The Lawns, and beyond, the shopfront of Horders.

Old Town, looking north-east from the tower of the Corn Exchange, 1930s. In the centre-background can be seen the Hermitage, a neo-Tudor early Victorian house built by C.A. Wheeler, a local chemist. In 1964 it became a short-stay home for elderly people, but after many years of neglect it was demolished in 1994 for redevelopment. When excavations took place on the site Saxon buildings were found.

A glimpse inside the private office of Brown & Plummer, wine merchants, Market Square, Old Town, 1923. The whole office appears to have changed little over many years, with its elegant furniture and cabinets. Now the whole building is vacated and rapidly becoming derelict.

Brown & Plummer cellars, Market Square, 1923. These brandy barrels and casks appear to have been in this position for many years.

The despatch area at Brown & Plummer, 1923. In the background is an advertisement for Worthington beer in casks or bottles, which can still be purchased today.

The cellars of Brown & Plummer, 1923. These cellars are said to be haunted by the ghost of a former cellarman, Stephen Lawrence, who drowned himself in the church pond. Champagne boxes are stored in neat rows (above), with bottled beers and casks (below).

Skaters at the Rink, Market Square, Old Town, 1911. The large hall of the Corn Exchange served as a roller-skating rink for several years before the First World War. In the background (above) can be seen an advertisement for Chandler Bros, the drapers in Wood Street, and also a notice prohibiting 'fast skating'. Roller-skating for men apparently involved being smartly dressed!

Skating on the Lawn Lakes, 1907. Known locally as the Park Ponds, these lakes were created in the mid-1700s when the park was laid out around the Goddard manor house.

Children queuing outside the Rink cinema in Market Square, Old Town, 1934. The cinema, formerly a skating rink (see p. 13), survived until the 1950s. The building was then used as a ballroom and a venue for wrestling promotions, and is now a bingo hall.

Courage Brewery buildings, High Street, c. 1970. This was formerly the North Wilts Brewery, which was owned by Richard Bowly. The premises were used by Courage until 1978. The whole site has now been redeveloped as the main local branch of Barclays Bank. During rebuilding work the words 'Bowly, Brewer' were found engraved over the central arch, and they have now been made into a feature of the building. (See also *Swindon in Old Photographs II*, p. 25.)

The entrance porch of the Goddard Arms, High Street, 1955. During repairs to the porch over the main entrance, the original arch over the doorway was uncovered, showing that the inn had been 'licenced to let post horses'. The system of carrying communications by messengers riding post horses was the origin of the postal service. An inn has stood here since the seventeenth century and it was known as the Crown until about 1810. (See also *Swindon in Old Photographs IV*, pp. 12–13.)

T.P. Stroud, carriage builder, Marlborough Road, *c.* 1905. This business was established here in 1841. The site is still involved with transport today, being Cowie's garage and parts department. The building on the right was then a veterinary surgeon's premises, and is now used as offices by Cowie's.

The Stroud family house, Marlborough Road, *c.* 1905. This building still stands today, next to Cowie's parts department, but the ornate porch and beautiful garden have long since disappeared.

Interior of the Little London Mission, Old Town, October 1925. This building, which stood opposite the parish church of Christ Church, on the corner of Church Road and Little London, was opened in 1902. The hall was equipped with a harmonium, and was used for regular Sunday services as well as a Sunday school. It was closed in 1949 and in 1953 was sold to local builders Pope Bros, who used it initially as a paint store. The metal cross on its roof still remains today.

Croft Road railway bridge, looking west. This photograph was taken in October 1961, after the closure of passenger services to Swindon Town station. The bridge was rebuilt shortly afterwards because of the increase of road traffic using the area.

Railwaymen tending the garden at the Swindon Town railway station, off Newport Street, c. 1946. No wonder the station had such a good reputation for its display of flower beds at this time!

Signalman Bill Walker, May 1929. He is looking out of the window of the Swindon Town 'B' signal cabin, near the Evelyn Street bridge.

This vintage Bentley motor car was owned by Reg Townsend, the licensee of the refreshment rooms on Swindon Town station, off Newport Street. The photograph was taken outside the station in about 1955, with Mr Townsend's mother at the wheel. Although the passenger service ceased in 1961, the refreshment rooms remained open, and were known locally as the 'Ghost Train'. They finally closed in February 1965.

F.B. Brown's shop front at 46 Prospect Place in 1968.

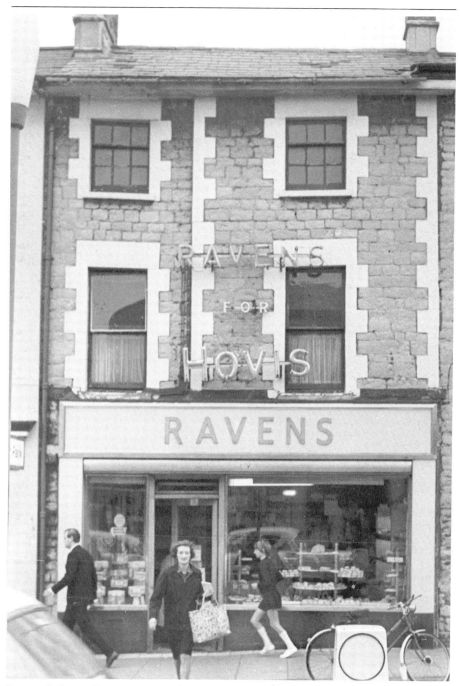

Ravens bakery, 89 Victoria Road, mid-1960s. It is now Aladdin's Cave, a Tandoori restaurant.

No. 6 branch of the New Swindon Industrial Co-operative Society Ltd, at 10 Kent Road, *c.* 1930. These premises were on the corner of Maidstone Road, and are currently the Kent Launderette. In the distance can be seen houses in Stafford Street.

Marlborough Road, looking north towards the High Street, 1981. On the left is the Cartwheel Café; beyond is the entrance to the cattle market, which closed in the late 1980s, and Gilbert's furniture store.

The Cartwheel Café, 18 Marlborough Road, 1981. In recent years these premises have been demolished to make way for new housing.

The rear of 'Farncombe', 24 Westlecott Road, *c*. 1935. At this time it was the home of Mr F. Collard, a local tailor whose business was in Victoria Road.

Ashford Road, looking east from the junction with Kent Road, *c*. 1910. (See also *Swindon in Old Photographs IV*, p. 19.)

61 Prospect Place, *c.* 1925. This was formerly the armoury of the Wiltshire Yeomanry. Recently parts of the structure have been demolished for further redevelopment.

These peaceful photographs of Croft Road were taken by Swindon photographer Fred C. Palmer, *c.* 1930. Croft Road, on the hill up to Old Town, is now one of the busiest routes into Swindon.

Section Two

THE RAILWAY
TOWN

*The GWR Mechanics' Institute, Emlyn Square, c. 1915. This opened in 1855 and
provided many facilities for GWR workers, including a theatre, a library, and reading and
lecture rooms. The building is now in a sad state of neglect but an action group, the New
Mechanics' Institute, was set up in Swindon in 1995 to preserve it. (See also* Swindon
in Old Photographs *I, pp. 31–2)*

This most unusual photograph shows K shop (coppersmiths and tinsmiths) night-shift workers in the GWR Works in 1919. Most photographs taken within the Works would be taken by professional photographers at this time, and for a worker to own a camera and a flash unit was rare. The K shop was known as Kc or Kt according to which trade was concerned.

A man feeding the pigeons inside the wheel shop, GWR Works, late 1930s.

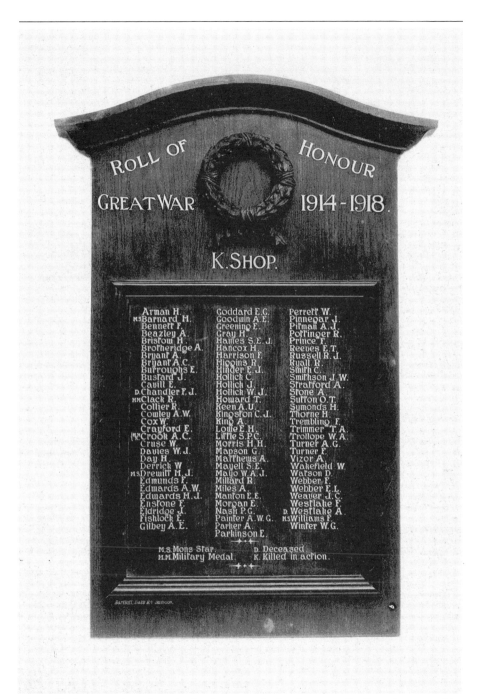

ROLL OF HONOUR

GREAT WAR 1914-1918.

K. SHOP.

Arman H.	Goddard E.G.	Perrett W.
M.S.Barnard H.	Goodwin A.E.	Pinnegar J.
Bennett F.	Greening E.	Pitman A.J.
Beazley A.	Gray H.	Pottinger R.
Bristow H.	Haines S.E.J.	Prince F.
Brotheridge A.	Hancox H.	Reeves E.T.
Bryant A.	Harrison F.	Russell R.J.
Bryant A.C.	Higgins R.	Ryall R.
Burroughs E.	Hinder E.J.	Smith C.
Bustard J.	Hollick C.	Smithson J.W.
Cavill E.	Hollick J.	Strafford A.
D.Chandler F.J.	Hollick W.J.	Stone A.
M.M.Clack R.	Howard T.	Sutton O.T.
Collier R.	Keen A.U.	Symonds H.
Cowley A.W.	Kingston C.J.	Thorne H.
Cox W.	King A.	Trembling F.
Crayford E.	Lowe E.H.	Trimmer T.A.
M.M.Crook A.C.	Little S.P.C.	Trollope W.A.
Cruse W.	Morris H.H.	Turner A.G.
Davies W.J.	Mapson G.	Turner F.
Day H.	Matthews A.	Vizor A.
Derrick W	Mayell S.E.	Wakefield W.
M.S.Drewitt H.J.	Majo W.A.J.	Watson D.
Edmunds F.	Millard R.	Webber F.
Edwards A.W.	Miles A.	Webber E.L.
Edwards H.J.	Manton E.E.	Weaver J.C.
Enstone F.	Morgan E.	Westlake F.
Eldridge J.	Nash P.G.	D.Westlake A.
Fishlock E.	Painter A.W.G.	M.S.Williams F.
Gilbey A.E.	Parker A.	Winter W.G.
	Parkinson E.	

M.S. Mons Star.　　　D. Deceased.
M.M.Military Medal.　K. Killed in action.

The Roll of Honour board inside the GWR Works for the men of K Shop (coppersmiths and tinsmiths) who served in the First World War.

Two views of the replica of the famous GWR 2–2–2 broad gauge locomotive, *North Star*, 1925. The replica was built in the GWR Works for the centenary of the Stockton & Darlington Railway. The original locomotive, built for the GWR by Robert Stephenson & Co. in 1837, had been cut up early in the century but many original parts were found lying around the Works and were used in the construction of the replica, which is now on view in the Swindon Railway Museum.

St Mark's Church, looking along Church Place from near the corner of Park Lane, 1906. The church was designed by George Gilbert Scott, and has just celebrated its 150th anniversary, having been consecrated in 1845.

The snow-covered gardens of the GWR Park in Faringdon Road, after the freak snowstorm which occurred in April 1908. St Mark's Church is in the distance.

Comic postcards depicting the scenes of the annual works holiday in the GWR, known as Trip, 1905. The first card shows the rush to board the coaches in the station sidings and the second shows the scene after the annual holiday, when the landlord's rent collector comes to collect the rent, only to find that nobody is at home! It should be remembered that, until 1938, this holiday was unpaid in the GWR.

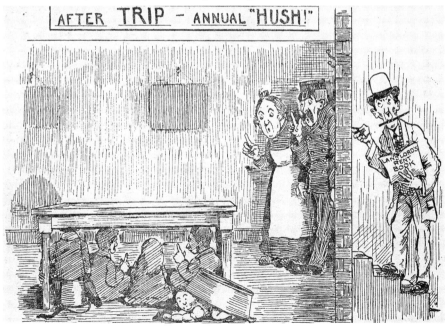

Brewing the tea at the GWR children's fête in 1911. These volunteers are filling the urns in the mess rooms, before transporting them to the marquees in the GWR Park, ready for the crowds. In this particular year they are reported to have brewed 680 gallons! The photograph was taken by local photographer William Hooper.

Emlyn Square, 1930s. The band is walking towards Faringdon Street (later Road). The building on the right, with 'C.R. Thomas' above the window, was the London Stout House, now known as the Gluepot public house.

Men leaving the GWR Works entrance in Rodbourne Road, 1905. (See *Swindon in Old Photographs I*, p. 41.) The tramcar shows an advertisement for Butlers Furniture in Bridge Street, which was claimed to be the cheapest and best.

The royal train, drawn by the Churchward 4–4–0 *City of Bath* (3433), at Rushey Platt, carrying the Prince and Princess of Wales to Plymouth, 14 July 1903. To the right is the loop to the Swindon Town station on the MSWJR line.

Manchester Road, looking east, with Salisbury Street on the left, *c.* 1919. Notice the excited children rushing to the fence to see the band, also the tram bringing up the rear.

Tramcar no. 4 leaving Manchester Road for Milford Street, *c.* 1905. Originally this part of the road, to the west of Corporation Street, was a dead-end known as Mill Street. A thoroughfare was provided for the tram system by demolishing part of the terrace on the east side of Wellington Street.

The route of the old North Wilts Canal, *c.* 1935. This was converted for use as a pedestrian and cycle path where it passed through the GWR Works, between Harcourt Road and Sheppard Street. It is still known by the locals as 'over the canal'.

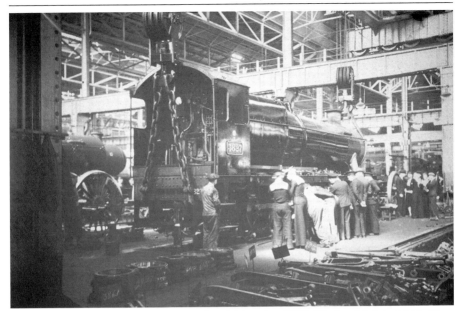

Members of the crew of HMS *Australia* visiting the GWR Works, 13 July 1945. They are examining a 2–8–0 locomotive (3827) in A Shop. Note the 'regulation' seven creases in the sailors' bell-bottom trousers.

Swindon running sheds in the 1950s. The two locomotives in view are (left) *Otterlington Hall* (6983), which was withdrawn from service in August 1965, and (right) *Albrighton Hall* (4984), which was withdrawn in September 1962.

Inside the GWR Works, August 1968. Diesel locomotives are being lifted by the overhead cranes in the sheds where once the 'Kings', 'Castles' and 'Halls' of the days of steam were photographed.

Swindon Junction Railway station platforms, April 1966. The section on the right has since been demolished.

Section Three

STREETS & SHOPS

The premises of J. Belcher, shipping agent, at 47 Faringdon Road, c. 1925. In the depression years after the First World War many local men and their families emigrated to the USA, Canada and Australia in search of a better life. Note the advertisements for household workers in Ontario; all the notices in the window refer to such opportunities.

Bindon's cash boot repairing depot at 14 Curtis Street, on the corner of Crombey Street, c. 1915. The two brothers who owned it are standing in the doorway. The advertisement in the window says, 'Have your boots repaired here – modern methods – up-to-date machines and best leather used'.

The shop front of J.J. Brown & Sons, makers of house furniture, 9–10 Station Road, c. 1910. This section of Station Road has been completely redeveloped in recent years with new office blocks being built.

The shop front of the Swindon Cash Drug Stores at 51 Fleet Street, *c.* 1910. The owner of the shop was E.V. Miles. In the days before the National Health Service, Mr Miles's own remedies were popular for minor ailments among those who could not benefit from the Railway Works medical fund. The premises are now used by the charity Age Concern.

The Swindon and District Co-operative Society chemists and pharmacy, at 44 Commercial Road, on the corner of Newhall Street, *c.* 1955. Formerly it was Miller's herbal stores. A modern office block now stands on this site.

The shop front of Drake Bros, 25 Tennyson Street, 1908. The shop was a family grocers and provision merchants. The adverts displayed in the window include G.P. Government Tea, McDougall's self-raising flour, Rowntree's cocoa and Maida's guaranteed pure butter.

Regent Street, looking north towards Bridge Street, *c*. 1930. The departmental store belonging to John Anstiss can be seen on the left.

Oriel Street, 1919. Mr and Miss Smith, with Miss Rose Smith (no relation), outside their general store and off-licence in Oriel Street, 1919. Rose was employed as a general help (housework and shop assistant) and lived in as one of the family. The shop was open seven days a week from 7 a.m. to 10 p.m., and Rose worked these hours with a one hour break for lunch and tea; she also had one half-day off per week, with an additional one hour on Sunday evening to attend St Luke's Church. For this she received 5s per week.

William Hooper's shop at 2 Market Street, *c.* 1904. The windows are filled with portraits and certificates for prize-winning photographs he had entered in national competitions. Hooper was responsible for many of the best photographs recording Swindon's history in this period.

The New Swindon Co-operative Society shops, 6–12 Fleet Street, *c.* 1953. These comprised menswear, footwear, shoe repairs, drapery, confectionery, bakery and grocery stores. Refurbished in 1950, these shops were built out from the original house fronts, which can be seen above the shops. The majority of these premises were completely demolished in later years and the Fleet Street open-air market now occupies the site. (For a view of the same area in the Victorian period, see *Swindon in Old Photographs III*, p. 100.)

The Co-operative Society's furniture store at 81 Regent Street, decorated for the coronation of Queen Elizabeth II in June 1953. This site is now part of the Marks & Spencer store. (For a glimpse of this site in earlier years see *Swindon in Old Photographs IV*, p. 92.)

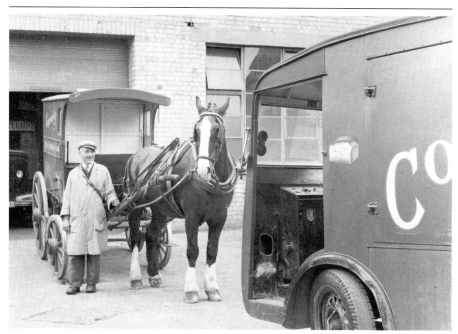

Fred Titchener and 'Punch', his horse, at the Co-operative Society Station Road bakery, 1953. At this time some deliveries were still made by horse-drawn vans.

The junction of Wootton Bassett Road with Kingsmill Road, looking towards the Running Horse public house, with Westcott Place to the right, c. 1920.

No. 7 branch of the New Swindon Industrial Co-operative Society Ltd, at 3 Park Lane, *c.* 1960. This was one of the first self-service grocery stores in Swindon. The premises are now the Esson Machinery and Tool Centre.

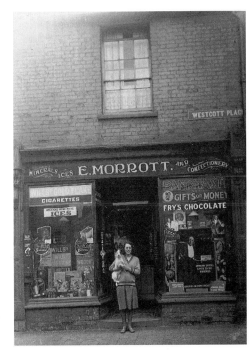

E. Morrott's shot front, at 178 Westcott Place, *c.* 1930. This shop was adjacent to the Ship Hotel and sold 'Minerals, Ices and Confectionary'.

A fire broke out at Franklin's, the decorators' merchant, in Cromwell Street, in July 1958. Next door can be seen Normans' shop front. This area is now under the Brunel Plaza shopping arcade off Canal Walk. When the area was redeveloped in 1970 Franklin's moved to premises in Shrivenham Road. It closed in recent years after over ninety years of business in the town.

Adolphus Dean, Gentlemen's Hairdresser, outside his shop at 34 Fleet Street, *c.* 1953.

Dean Street, looking west, *c.* 1910. On the left is the junction with George Street. Note the ornate Victorian stonework of the bay windows and porches of the houses on the left, much of which has survived to the present time.

Jennings Street, 1926. This general store at no. 39, on the corner with Grove Street, was owned by Mr and Mrs Newman. Outside are Mrs Newman's mother with her grandchildren. In the background outside no. 37 is Mrs Sarah Lewis with her grandchildren, Peggy and Dorothy. Later, the shop was taken over by Mrs Brookman, and then changed to a fish and chip shop.

No. 2 branch of the New Swindon Industrial Co-operative Society Ltd, at 2 Rodbourne Road, 1911. This branch had just moved from the opposite side of Rodbourne Road. Second from the right is Thomas Langcaster, the manager. (For another view see *Swindon in Old Photographs IV*, p. 95.)

No. 3 branch of the New Swindon Industrial Co-operative Society Ltd, at 134 Cricklade Road, *c.* 1950. Serving the customers are Harry Brinkworth and Mac Hayward. Note the cash 'cup-and-pull' system in operation. These premises still house a Co-op grocery store today.

The official opening of the New Swindon Industrial Co-operative Ltd branch at 531 Cricklade Road in 1938. The lower photograph shows the interior of the shop on the day it opened. There is still a Co-op store today in Clive Parade.

Looking up Victoria Road from the junction with Groundwell Road, *c.* 1960. On the left, on the corner with Durham Street, can be seen the Victoria garage. (See p. 65.)

The interior of the showrooms at W.J. Moran's electrical shop at 153 Victoria Road, 1927. This family business lasted until recent years on this site. These premises are now being used by Austin's Leisure/Electrical. (See also *Swindon in Old Photographs I*, p. 69.)

Section Four

INDUSTRIES &
LOCAL BUSINESS

Moredon power station photographed from the
fields in front of Akers Way, 1956. A new housing
development now stands on this site. The road
bridge which crossed the MSWJR line close to the
cooling towers of the power station has also been
demolished.

Lower Eastcott Farm, Corporation Street, *c.* 1896. The Swindon Corporation electricity works were built on this site in 1903. (See also *Swindon in Old Photographs I*, p. 88.)

Aerial view of the New Swindon Gas Works in Gypsy Lane, Gorse Hill, *c.* 1915. The gas works transferred here from Queen Street in 1893.

Moredon Power Station, 1966. The original electricity generating station in Corporation Street (see *Swindon in Old Photographs III*, p. 74), was replaced by the Moredon Power Station in 1929. This was eventually taken out of use in 1973 and the cooling towers and chimney demolished in 1979. The area is now covered by the Pembroke Park housing estate.

The junction of the GWR main line with the loop to the former MSWJR (right), at Rushey Platt, photographed from the bridge on the MSWJR, 1961. The 'Old Town' line was closed to passenger traffic in September 1961. On the right are the Midland sawmills of James Davies (formerly E.J. Barnes).

A traction engine pulling a load of tree trunks at Rushey Platt, the site of Barnes' sawmills, in the early 1900s. The photographer was H. Hemmins of Victoria Street, Swindon.

An early crane engine at Barnes' sawmills at Rushey Platt, *c.* 1886. The lifting gear on the front of this engine would have saved a lot of the man-handling of the huge tree trunks.

The Burrell traction engine *King George V*, owned by E.J. Barnes & Sons, pictured at Rushey Platt sawmills with a heavy load of tree trunks.

The E.J. Barnes & Son traction engine *Walter Long* pulling three trailers full of bark from the saw mills at Rushey Platt in 1905. The power of these engines was amazing considering that each of these trailers weighed over three tons empty. The photograph was taken by William Hooper, the famous Swindon photographer.

Interior of the Barnes' sawmills at Rushey Platt, *c.* 1899. This photograph was taken by the husband and wife Swindon photographers George and Ada Stone, who had premises in Faringdon Street and also at Wood Street.

Okus Quarries, *c.* 1912. The limestone workings later became part of the Bradley yard, with the limestone still being used, but now in the production of mortar for their building sites. This continued until the council purchased the land for Commonweal School in the early 1970s.

The main post office at Regent Circus, *c.* 1910. To the right is the wall of large stone villa, the home of the well-known Swindon surgeon, Dr Lavery, for many years. (See also *Swindon in Old Photographs IV*, pp. 62 and 133.)

SWINDON

Established 30 Years.

EVERYTHING FOR YOUR MOTOR

Telephone : Nos. 266/7 Swindon.   Telegrams : " Skurray, Swindon."

A 1929 advertisement for Skurray's Garage, at 30–32 High Street. The Co-op superstore now stands on this site.

Skurray's showrooms in Old Town, opposite the Market Square, 1929. The lower photograph shows the interior, with gleaming Buick cars for sale. The prices of these cars ranged from £550 (for the 23–75 model) to £398 (for the 20–60 model). Notice the elegant wooden panelling inside the showrooms.

Another interior view of Skurray's showrooms, in 1929. The car is a Buick.

An accident outside 42 County Road, *c.* 1950. A Co-operative Society building department lorry has collided with a wall and gatepost. This view is looking north towards Gorse Hill.

These lorries, parked on the side of the road at Stow-on-the-Wold hill in 1937, belonged to the Swindon family firm, Edwards, still famous for their fun-fairs. Standing by the Ford V8 car are Bob Edwards and Peter O'Season (whose mother was one of the Lyons tea family). The first lorry in the line was an Armstrong Sawyer. Edwards' fun-fair company still operates from Ferndale Road to this day.

Edwards' lorries on the road again in 1937. The Armstrong Sawyer lorry at the front carried the fuel needed for the lorries (the tank held 500 gallons). The fuel was purchased in bulk at 7d per gallon, 2d per gallon cheaper than usual. The first wagon advertises the 'latest Rytecraft–Air Flow cars'.

A proud Bob Edwards poses in front of a line-up of Edwards' lorries, just after the Second World War. On the road they had a top speed of 20 mph, and each weighed over 7³/₄ tons. Each was given a name, and those in the picture are 'The Moonraker', 'Duchess of Gloucester' and 'The Queen of the Cotswolds'.

Edwards' traction engine *Earl Kitchener* with a young admirer in the 1970s. This engine was originally purchased in 1920 from Hills (the Swindon building supplies firm) for the sum of 5s down and 1s per week for the remainder. It was certainly a good investment as it was still being used fifty years later. In the background is a Austin 1800 motor car.

GET YOUR NEW
MORRIS

DIRECT FROM THE MAIN DEALERS

The Victoria Garage

PHONE 205

Victoria Road, Swindon

PRICES FROM £130

HERE IS THE NEW MORRIS-OXFORD
15 H.P.   SIX CYLINDER.   FABRIC SALOON.

PRICE £285

An advertisement for the Victoria Garage, 20 Victoria Road, 1929. The premises, at the corner of Durham Street, are now occupied by Machine Mart.

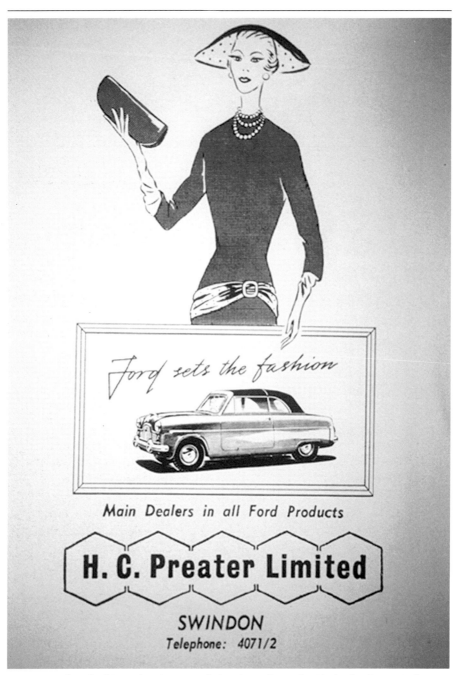

Ford sets the fashion

Main Dealers in all Ford Products

H. C. Preater Limited

SWINDON
Telephone: 4071/2

A more modern looking advertisement, dating from the early 1950s, for Preater's Garage, Princes Street, with the quote 'Ford sets the fashion'. This garage later became Walker Jackson's and now Cowie's motor vehicles sales rooms stand on the site. (See also p. 153.)

An early Sentinel lorry owned by E. Hill and Sons (haulage contractors) of Swindon, *c.* 1924. Lorries with solid tyres had a speed limit of 12 mph, which was reduced to 5 mph if pulling a trailor. Hill's telephone number was Swindon 212.

A later Sentinel lorry, also owned by E. Hill, *c.* 1925. The company is now advertising bricks, sand, ballast and cement on the sides of the wagon. The advancement in the tyres from the lorry shown above is obvious, and allowed the speed limit to rise to 20 mph.

Emily Peart in front of W.D. & H.O. Wills' tobacco factory in Colbourne Street, 29 June 1934. This area is now covered by the Tesco superstore and car park. (See also *Swindon in Old Photographs IV*, p. 56.)

Hector V. Slade, chairman of the Garrard Engineering & Manufacturing Co. Ltd from 1945. The factory opened in Swindon in 1919 with 40 employees but by 1950 it employed 1,400 people on several local sites. The company was renowned throughout the world for its high quality automatic record changers, spring and electric gramophone motors, as well as pick-ups and clocks.

Fire at Garrards in Newcastle Street, photographed at 10 p.m. on 21 March 1958; at this time the fire was at its height. It had broken out in the despatch block at 9 p.m. and swept through the new single-storey assembly building (pictured here), and also the three-storey despatch building which overlooked the canal site. Water to fight the fire was pumped from Queens Park Lake some distance away, as the wartime static water supply no longer existed.

These two photographs show the inspection area buildings and the record changer department the morning after the fire at Garrard's. The damage was extensive but the clean up started immediately. The mass of burnt, tangled girders and twisted assembly lines was all cleared by Garrard employees with the help of Bradleys workers by Sunday the 23rd. The damaged and twisted record decks were loaded on to lorries supplied by Bradleys and removed to Bradley's yard in Okus.

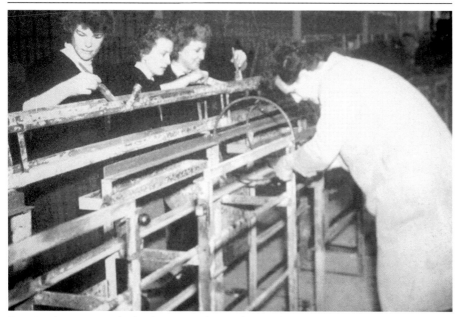

By Monday 24 March the first reconditioned assembly lines for Garrard's were being rebuilt and painted at Rodbourne Industrial Estate. More straightened production lines arrived later that afternoon from the Vickers factory at South Marston and were immediately rebuilt by the employees.

The sub-assembly lines at Garrard's, back in full production after the re-building, 1958.

H.M. Queen Elizabeth II signing the visitors book at Garrard's factory, Newcastle Street, 5 November 1971. She is being escorted by Mr Maurice Eley (centre), and Sir John Clark.

Garrard's senior shop stewards, June Little, Bill Baxter and Mary Rogers, December 1975. Early in January 1976 they were sent on a fact-finding tour to the United States (at the time the USA took 30 per cent of the firm's output). This involved seeing the competition that the firm faced and the problems that Garrard's were facing in the world market. These problems eventually proved insurmountable and in February 1982 the company announced that, for economic reasons, all manufacturing activities would cease on 1 May 1982.

The junction of the Highworth Branch railway line with the main line to the right, c. 1960. In the background is the recently opened Pressed Steel factory.

C Building of the Pressed Steel factory under construction, 1960. The land for the factory was purchased in December 1954, and the first two presses were in operation by December 1955, with the first stamping being completed on New Year's Eve, although the building itself was not finished until July 1956. C Building was the third major production unit on the site, and included both press and assembly shops; the floor area was in excess of 450,000 square feet.

The Duke of Edinburgh visited the Pressed Steel factory in April 1961; here he is being shown a power press working.

The factory policeman checking out a load of car bodies, ready for the journey to Cowley, Oxford, outside the Pressed Steel factory gates, Bridge End Road, late 1950s.

RODBOURNE & MOREDON

Elm Cottage, Cheney Manor Road. At the end of the nineteenth century the local midwife lived here. Later this property was demolished to make way for the building of the Church Hall.

Morris Street, Rodbourne, looking east, 1917. Roadworks are taking place around the lamp post on the left.

Primrose Eley (right) and her sister-in-law Olive Eley, standing at the gate of 'Westview', Church Walk North, Rodbourne, in 1934. (See *Swindon in Old Photographs IV*, p. 70.)

Whitworth Road, looking towards the brow from the Rodbourne Arms, *c.* 1920. This lovely quiet view is in complete contrast to the present day heavy traffic now using this road.

Whitworth Road, 1930s. This is the view from the brow, looking towards Stratton crossroads, with the buildings now shaping the road as we know it today.

Harvest time at Manor Farm, Rodbourne Cheney, 1929. Albert Harvey was the farmer here until his retirement in 1935, and Harvey Grove is named after him. The tower of St Mary's Church can be seen in the background.

Threshing wheat at Manor Farm, 1929. The farmhouse here was demolished in 1963.

Mr and Mrs Eley pose with their children, Violet, Bill, Glad and Minnie at Moredon in 1912. The windows on the right-hand side of the building belong to the Moredon Bakehouse.

Moredon Home Guard unit pictured outside the farmhouse at Maundrell's Farm (opposite The Boundary House public house), during the First World War. Back row, left to right: Mr J.H.C. Maundrell (the local farmer), Major Lyford, Mr Manners, J. People, Jim Beasant, Arthur Eley, -?-, Mark Howse, Mark Beasant, G. Perry, Mr Varney, -?-, Mr Loder. Front row: James Caswell, Mr Robins, Bill Beasant, Mr Gibbs, Jobie Lewis, -?-, Ebur Titcombe, Ted Weaving. Some of the rifles in this picture are Martini-Henrys, dating from the 1880s.

Moredon Road, looking west from near Rodbourne Cheney primary school, *c.* 1920. Moredon Veterinary Clinic now occupies one of the houses to the right.

The Fox and Hounds public house, Haydon Wick, *c.* 1910. Opened as a beerhouse between 1830 and 1851 (when it was owned by a farmer), it was then taken over by Reed Bros, and later became a Bowly's brewery house in about 1880, before being taken over by Simonds and finally Courage.

Reuben Hiett of Moredon, Swindon and Highworth carrier, *c.* 1905. This photograph may have been taken outside the Jesmond House Hotel at Highworth.

Leila Cox, daughter of the landlord, Arthur Cox, pictured outside the Fox and Hounds public house, Haydon Wick, 1927. She used to give piano lessons to pupils on the piano in the bar.

Section Six

COMMUNITY LIFE
IN SWINDON

*Seated in the middle of this group of ladies is 'Grandmother Bristow' (formerly Susan
Rourke, a Canadian), surrounded by family members, c. 1900. Back row, left to right:
Margaret (married George Moulding), Annie (married George Haydon), Susan (remained a
spinster), Phoebe (married George Box), Mary (married John Norris). Middle row: Mrs
Day, 'Grandmother Bristow', Mrs Buckingham. Front row: Annie (married John Bristow),
Gertrude (married George Bristow). As with all photographs taken in this period, posing
for the camera seems to be a very serious business.*

Members of the Ferndale Road Methodist Church enjoying a summer outing with their families, *c.* 1910. The chapel was opened in 1907, and an extension built on to the main building was opened in September 1960; this was partly financed by the sale of the Regent Street Church.

Senior members of the Ferndale Road Methodist Church on an outing, *c.* 1910.

All Saints' Church choir, *c.* 1915. This photograph was taken outside the temporary church built in Southbrook Street in 1908; this became the Parish Hall in 1938, and was demolished in 1976. In the centre is the Revd Ernest Topley, who served as priest-in-charge from 1908 to 1916 and finished his ministry as Vicar of Greenhithe, Kent. The red cape he is wearing is still kept at All Saints' and is used occasionally at services. The brass cross is also still in regular use at the church, as is the white banner, which has been re-made without the inscription. Gilbert Taylor is second from the left in the back row; Harry Pitman is third from the left in the second row from the back; Arthur Pitman is second from the right in the front row. All Saints' was at first a mission district closely associated with St Mark's, but was formed into a separate parish in 1929. The present church was built in 1937.

The Railway Mission bible class, *c.* 1910. The Railwaymen's Christian Association established itself in the town in the 1880s, meeting in the Swimming Baths hall or the Mechanics' Institute. In 1903 a Mission Room was built in Wellington Street, on the corner of Milford Street. Several generations of Swindon railwaymen attended the mission which was run and organized almost entirely by women up to 1937. It was destroyed by fire in 1979 and office blocks now stand on this site. (See also *Swindon in Old Photographs III*, p. 102.)

Children's outing from Regent's Place Gospel Hall (Christian Brethren), 1905. The photographer William Hooper had been involved in the actual design of the building when it was built in 1899. One of the most popular places for church outings was Charlton Ponds near Purton.

Students and teachers at Clarence Street School, 1923–4. Included in the group are J. May, A. Ellis, C.M. Jones, S.C. Wilkins, J.O. Maisey, A.E. Dean, Brenda Price, Kate Robins, Nora Whiting, W.G. Ball, Esther Little, Gwen Scott, M.J. Potter, Madelaine Vick, Mabel Dale, George F. Ashworth, Audrey Jones, Thelma Truscott, Mabel Payne, Irene Taylor, P. Bevan, Ethel Teall, Freda Mason, K. Adams and L. Harper.

The presentation of the first prize for the 1929 Swindon and North Wilts. Victoria Hospital Carnival draw. This took place in November 1930 at the showrooms of the Swindon Motor Company. The deputy mayor, Alderman G.H. Hunt (who had been mayor at the time of the draw) presented Mrs F.A. Bristow of Manchester Road with a four-seater Triumph Super Seven Tourer. Her son Frank is sitting behind the wheel; her husband, who actually won the prize, was unable to attend the presentation. Besides winning the car, he had also won the second prize, a gentleman's suit, valued at £7 7s. He had shown his appreciation of winning both prizes by presenting the hospital fund with a cheque for £10 10s. Twenty-two other prizes had been won and the hospital benefited to the sum of £2,200 from the money raised.

The nativity play by Sanford Street Congregational Church Sunday School, *c.* 1937. In the back row are Betty Summers, Audrey Doell, Margaret Scott, Jose Richen and Evelyn Doughty. In the middle row are Jim Richards, Philip Webb, Chris Kent, Stan Richards, Jean Richen, Margaret Kent, Peter Matthews, Alan Curtis, Geoff Painter and Philip Hammond. In the front row are ? Hawkins, ? Hawkins, Alan Bunce and Joyce Doell.

Sanford Street Congregational Church Sunday School choir at Trowbridge, 1937. Back row, left to right: Ray Curtis, Chris Kent, Jean Richen, ? Richards, Barbara Howell. Middle row: Geoff Painter, ? Painter, Margaret Kent, ? Hemmings, Margaret Scott. Front row: John Summerhayes, Ron Webb, Alan Matthews, Stan Richards, Joyce Richen. The conductor was Mrs Bullock (left) and the pianist Mrs Jones (right).

Bob Menham with his daughter Betty in the back garden of the Castle Hotel, *c.* 1915. Born in Tynemouth (Northumberland) in 1871, he had enlisted in the 3rd Volunteer Battalion, West Yorkshire Regiment, and in 1890 transferred to the 3rd Battalion Grenadier Guards. He was in the Grenadier Guards regimental rugby team and also played in goal for the regimental football team at the Croft (Swindon Town's home ground at this time). After extending his service for a further period in 1893, he continued playing football and was 'bought out' of the army by Everton Football Club for the sum of £18 to play professional football. He played in the 1897 Cup Final at the Crystal Palace when Aston Villa defeated Everton 3–2 (before a crowd of 79,000). From Everton he transferred to play for Wigan and in 1898 joined Swindon Town. These were hard financial times for the club and in 1901, as captain of the club, Menham wrote a letter appealing for funds for the club to continue (the players for a period having collected only half their regular wages). He was forced to retire in the 1902/3 season owing to failing eyesight. After serving as the steward of the West Swindon Club he became the landlord of the Castle Hotel, with his wife Bessie. During this period he was vice-president of Swindon and District Licensed Victuallers Association (1902–10), and later president (1910–20). He had also become a director of the football club, and also a town councillor; in 1911 he was chairman of Swindon and District Hospital Board. After leaving the Castle Hotel in 1928 the family ran a restaurant for a number of years. Menham died in January 1945. The one remaining mystery is his FA Cup loser's medal, which was lost in 1909 in a field adjoining the Black Horse, and has never been found.

Members of the Ferndale Road working men's club pictured with their trophies after winning the Victory, Dominoes and Whist Cups in the 1924/5 season. This photograph by L. Maylott shows J. Comley, J. Tavener, H. March, T. New, W. Henley (president), W. Hunt, T. Haskins, J. Moulding, G. Thorne, M. Beale, E. Rogers, W. Lintern (secretary), C. Lewis, E. Stratton, W. Neatse, and I. Carpenter.

Girls fom Nicholson's raincoat factory in County Road standing proudly in front of their decorated float with their collecting tins ready, before a carnival, 1932.

Interior of the Gorse Hill Baptist Church, Cricklade Road, shortly after its opening in 1904. (See *Swindon in Old Photographs IV*, p. 65.)

Members of the 2nd Swindon Troop Boy Scouts in camp near Ashbury, *c.* 1912. Seated is District Commissioner W.R. Bird, who was also involved in the formation of the 4th Swindon Group. This group also includes F.A. Warminger, who was the patrol leader. The Scouts always received a great welcome from the villagers at Ashbury and would march into the village headed by the Scouts bugle and drum band.

The Tyler brothers in Scout uniform, 1914. Maurice, Norman and Eric (left to right) were members of the 2nd Swindon Troop. The family lived at the time at 1 Westlecot Road and their father had been the Secretary for North Wilts. Scouts from the time the movement had started in the town.

Young members of the 2nd Swindon Troop photographed at Colonel Calley's estate at Burderop Park in 1910. Left to right: Arthur Blackman, Frank Brittain, Norman Tyler, Bertie Tyler. By this time over 460 boys were registered as Scouts in the Swindon district, and there were also troops in Wootton Bassett, Stratton, Rodbourne and Blunsdon as well as the four in Swindon.

Members of the 2nd Swindon Troop en route to a weekend camp at Burderop Park in 1911. Colonel Calley was a great supporter of the local Scouts and regular camps took place on the north side of the house. The trek cart the scouts are hauling could be quickly dismantled for carrying across streams or rough ground.

Two photographs by Hooper of the GWR Park, 18 June 1910. Lieutenant General Sir R.S.S. Baden-Powell KCB, KCVO (later Lord Baden-Powell), visited the town to view the progress made by the local Boy Scout movement since the inception of his scheme in 1908. In the top photograph, he is seen reviewing the march past of the bugle, fife and drum band led by Bandmaster A. Johnson. The Boy Scout movement had been started in Swindon by Mr Spry, who was a Petty Officer in the Naval Reserve. At the time of Baden-Powell's visit there were about 460 boys in the Swindon District which included Wootton Bassett, Stratton, Rodbourne and Blunsdon, as well as the Swindon troops. In the lower picture, the Malmesbury, Marlborough, Stratton and Swindon troops are demonstrating bridge building and ambulance work. Large crowds came to watch the review and other activities; adults paid 6d each, with children half price, to enter the Park.

Boy Scouts building a bonfire off Quarry Road, ready for celebrations of the coronation of King George V and Queen Mary in June 1911.

Leaders of the 2nd Swindon Troop, pictured in 1914. Left to right: Sidney Dowse, W.R. Bird (District Commissioner), Harry Brittain, Lieutenant Grainger. The latter lost his life in action during the First World War. The troop met at the Maxwell Street School one night a week for drill. Mr Bird, who lived at 125 Goddard Avenue, was the chief chemist in the GWR Works.

Boys and staff from Swindon schools and Marlborough College attending the annual camp at Marlborough, 1933. The Marlborough–Swindon Camp Club was a social experiment that developed out of the comradeship between men of all classes of society who served at the front in the First World War. A classics master at Marlborough College, H.L.O. Flecker, inspired with the idea of trying to break down the class barriers which marred British life, suggested to the Master of Marlborough College, Dr Cyril Norwood, that fifty boys from Swindon's elementary schools should be invited to spend a week's summer holiday at the college. Dr Norwood wrote to Swindon Education Committee in 1922 proposing the first camp and this suggestion was accepted. Mr A.E. Bullock, a teacher at Jenning's Street School, and later headmaster of Sanford Street School, became the scheme's first secretary. Boys were chosen from each of Swindon's elementary schools, and on arrival at Marlborough they were split into five 'houses', each consisting of ten Swindon boys and two from the college. Most of the week was spent in competitive games. The scheme grew rapidly over the next few years, with the number of Swindon boys visiting the college being increased to ninety each year. Apart from the week's camp at Marlborough, meetings of the club took place throughout the year in Swindon, firstly in a shed in a garden in Springfield Road, and then, from 1929, in the former offices of the MSWJR off Newport Street in Old Town (now occupied by the North Wilts. Sanitary & Heating Co. Ltd), where they remained until 1950, except during the war years. The club then moved to the Marlborough Room in Aylesbury Street in the grounds of St John's Church. Unfortunately the club and the camps had ceased by the 1960s, along with much of the idealism that its founders had started off with after the 'war to end all wars'.

Section Seven

EVENTS &
CELEBRATIONS

The Tram Centre, at the junction of Bridge Street and Fleet Street, on the opening day of
the tram service, 22 September 1904. There are several photographs of this event by
Hooper, the Swindon photographer. The clock in the wall above the shops on the right was
used by the trams as the official time-piece; it is still there today, although in a slightly
different position. (See Swindon in Old Photographs *I, p. 89.)*

A victim of the infamous tramcar disaster being lifted out of the overturned vehicle, 1 June 1906. Tramcar no. 11's brakes had failed, causing it to run out of control down Victoria Road; at the bottom of the hill, on reaching the curve, it became derailed and turned over on its side. Five passengers died and thirty others were badly injured. (See also *Swindon in Old Photographs I*, pp. 99 and 100.)

Huge crowds gathered in the street outside the Town Hall, waiting to hear the election results, *c.* 1910. At this time great political upheaval was taking place in the country.

Fire broke out at the Great Western Hotel in the early hours of the morning, on 29 July 1913. In this Hooper photograph firemen are sorting through the remains of the garage area (where the fire originated). (See *Swindon in Old Photographs IV*, p. 111.)

Crashed aircraft at Lydiard Tregoze, 10 May 1913. The pilot, an officer from the Flying School at Netheravon, lost his way after leaving Swindon and landed in a field at Lydiard Tregoze. Attempting to take off again, however, the aircraft turned over and was wrecked. Luckily neither the pilot nor his pupil were injured. (See *Swindon in Old Photographs II*, p. 88.)

Looking towards the Town Hall, heavily decorated for the Coronation of King George V and Queen Mary in June 1911. On the left stands the Rifleman's Hotel, and on the right is the Baptist Tabernacle.

This Leyland Titan bus, operated by Swindon Corporation Transport, decorated in red, white and blue for the Coronation of King George VI and Queen Elizabeth, is pictured near Evelyn Street bridge, Marlborough Road, in 1937. The driver is Arthur Hughes and the conductor Bert Manning. On the railway embankment in the background can be seen GWR 0–6–0 tank engine (7782), near the goods transfer shed.

Front view of the same bus, this time looking towards the junction with Evelyn Street bridge, also in 1937. Driver Arthur Hughes is on the left and Bert Manning the conductor is on the right.

Princess Elizabeth outside the Town Hall on 15 November 1950. She visited Swindon to officially open Swindon's Garden of Remembrance and the Moredon playing fields, and also visited the GWR Works (the carriage paint shop, trimming shop and the sewing room). Here she is inspecting the Guard of Honour by members of four local Territorial units.

Crowds gathered in Groundwell Road to watch Princess Elizabeth pass on her way to open the Garden of Remembrance, 15 November 1950.

Swindon Junction station, 23 July 1954. They are busily cleaning the red carpet ready for the official visit of HM Queen Elizabeth II to Swindon. She was on her way to Wroughton Airfield to present new colours to the 1st, 2nd, and 4th (TA) Battalions of the Royal Welch Fusiliers, in her role of Colonel-in-Chief of the Regiment. Before the Queen's visit a big clean-up campaign took place; this included corporation dust-carts touring the official route using loudspeakers telling people, 'Put your litter in a bin. Your rags and salvage keep down the rates.' The Royal Train duly arrived, pulled by *Hartlebury Castle* (7033), into Platform 1, beautifully decorated with flowers. The Queen was greeted by Lord Oaksey, Major C.E. Awdry (High Sherriff of Wiltshire), Lieutenant-Colonel H.A. Golden (Chief Constable), Cllr A. Bennett (Mayor of Swindon), Ald. H. Gardner (Deputy Mayor), Mr D. Murray John (Town Clerk) and their respective wives. Also presented was Mr E. Sharples, the station-master, as well as other railway officials involved in the visit. After this a bouquet was presented to the Queen by five-year-old Carol Moss of Morris Street. Facing the official car in the lower photograph is mace-bearer Fred Titcombe who has the mace reversed; this is only allowed when a reigning monarch is within the borough. The Mayor travelled with the Queen to the Borough boundary, where he took his leave and returned to his own car at the rear of the official procession, which then continued to Wroughton Airfield.

The official procession waiting to leave Swindon Junction station, 23 July 1954.

Crowds gathered outside the Queen's Tap pub opposite the station, awaiting the Queen's arrival in July 1954. Note the old wooden taxi rank building in the background.

The Bath and West Show, Broome Manor Lane, May 1957. The Royal Canadian Mounted Police (*right*) proved to be a major attraction, especially to the young boys of the town. Following the gun carriage (*below*) are the King's Troop of the Royal Horse Artillery, about to enter the arena to perform their musical drive.

Faringdon Road, 21 May 1967. The elephants of Billy Smart's Circus are on their way to Westcott Place recreation ground, where the circus was based while in town. The route they took, with the procession leaving the station at 2.30 pm, was Station Road, Wellington Street, Milford Street, Fleet Street, Faringdon Road, Westcott Place and then Wootton Bassett Road. There were two shows a day and the prices ranged from 4s 6d to 21s.

The Town Gardens dome during a Miss TWW contest, 22 July 1967. TWW was the independent television company for the area at the time. There were usually about seven heats within the broadcasting area, each held in one of the larger towns, with the winners reaching the final from which a Miss TWW was selected. The Swindon heat was won by Mrs Iris Styles of Park South, a 23-year-old mother. There were many different contests for local beauties to enter – even McIlroy's had a beauty contest from which a Miss Elegance was selected.

Section Eight

SPORT &
ENTERTAINMENT

'Epitaph' to Swindon Town Football Club, after their 2–0 defeat in the semi-final of the
FA Cup on Tottenham's ground, against Newcastle United in 1910. In the early rounds
they had defeated Crystal Palace, Burnley, Tottenham and, to reach the semi-final,
Manchester City. The players in the semi-final were L. Skiller, H. Kay, J. Walker,
B. Tout, C. Bannister, B. Silto, B. Jefferson, H. Fleming, F. Wheatcroft, A. Bown,
J. Lavery. The photograph was taken at Bridge Street Club.

The famous Swindon Victoria FC team from the 1920/1 season. The Vics were formed in 1900 and became one of the best local sides between the two world wars. But in this season the team became nationally known for their exploits in reaching the FA Amateur Cup Final. Starting in the preliminary rounds, it took them ten matches to reach this stage – with 34 goals for and only 6 against. The final was played at Ayresome Park, Middlesbrough, before a crowd of 25,000 against Bishop Auckland who won 4–2 (3–1 at half-time). The team for the final was Weston (goalkeeper), Saunders and Poole (full backs), Roberts, Cooper and Summers (half backs), Rees, Blunsden, Eggleton, Dawson and Chivers (forwards), with Jones and Smith as reserves. The scorers for the Vics were Saunders and Poole (pen.). Other players in the team were Painter, Done and Glaze. It took the professionals of Bath City to beat the Vics – after a replay – to stop them progressing in the FA Cup as well. Besides these cup exploits they also won both the Wiltshire League and Wiltshire Cup. Several of the team, including the centre half, Reggie Cooper, left the club and became semi-professionals with Trowbridge Town. Reggie also played in the Football League with Swindon Town from 1922 to 1928. The Vics continued to enjoy success, on one occasion in the 1930s reaching the 4th qualifying round of the FA Cup, defeating the professionals of Bath City in the process. After the Second World War the team never achieved the same success and finally disbanded some years ago when they amalgamated with Malmesbury to form Malmesbury Victoria.

Celebrations in Gorse Hill in March 1969, as the coach carrying the victorious Swindon Town players toured the town showing the fans the League Cup trophy. They had defeated the famous Arsenal 3–1 after extra time, with Roger Smart and Don Rogers scoring the goals. Holding the cup are Stan Harland (captain) and Danny Williams (manager). In the lower photograph, looking across the junction of Ferndale Road with Cricklade Road, Gorse Hill, the crowds were dispersing after watching the coach carrying the victorious Town players pass by.

Swindon Schools Football Team, season 1955/6. This team reached the semi-finals of the English Schools Trophy; they also won the Cabot Cup, and the Berks, Bucks and Oxon Cup. Back row, left to right: D. Munden (Commonweal), R. Goulding (Ferndale), A. Dobson (Sanford), M. Marks (Upper Stratton), D. McIver (Upper Stratton), D. Reeves (Commonweal), A. Puffett (Pinehurst), R. Bushel (Headlands), D. Hyner (Commonweal). Front row: R. Woodruff (Upper Stratton), D. Gardener (Sanford), A. Bates (Sanford), Mr F. Coleman (Manager), D. Hobbs (Headlands), A. Wall (Headlands), M. Gibbs (Moredon).

Swindon Speedway supporters pose in front of their coach en route to an away fixture at Raleigh (in Essex), August bank holiday, 1951. The Swindon club was formed in 1949 and took over the fixtures of the disbanded Hull team that season.

DIVING BOARD, COATE WATER, SWINDON.

Coate Water, with the diving stage in use, late 1930s. The new concrete diving stage, which was officially opened at a gala on 22 June 1935, was erected to the design of Mr J.B.L. Thompson (the Borough Surveyor) in accordance with the regulations of the Federation Internationale de Natation Amateur. Miss Cicely Cousins, winner of the ASA High Diving Championship in 1934, gave a diving exhibition at the opening.

Coate Water swimming pool, *c*. 1950s. In recent years this has been redeveloped as a paddling pool for children.

Rodbourne Lake, *c.* 1950. Fred Plaum, the owner, is riding an experimental converted bicycle with floats, whose inventor hoped to convince Mr Plaum to place an order for several to be used by the public.

Rodbourne Lake was known as Plaum's Pits by the locals, and in the early 1950s it was a very popular place with Swindon people in the summer. Here youngsters on the floating stage pose for the camera.

The paddling pool at Rodbourne Lake was obviously very popular with very young children. In the background is the diving stage to the big lake.

This is thought to be Fred Plaum watching the digging of the small pool at Rodbourne Lake in 1947. The two men pushing the wheelbarrow are Charles Rumble (a fireman on the GWR), and Bill Meredith (a milkman with the Co-op); both of them had the reputation of being Pinehurst 'strongmen' in the local area.

THE REGENT

REGENT CIRCUS   ..   ..   SWINDON   ..   ..   'PHONE **750.**

Under the direct control of THE PROVINCIAL CINEMATOGRAPH THEATRES LTD.

Manager   ..   ..   ..   A. G. HARMAN

CONTINUOUS

NIGHTLY

6 to 10-30

MATINEES

DAILY

AT 2-30

Grand Opening Monday, September 16th, 1929

AT 7-30 P.M   DOORS 7 P.M.

By HIS WORSHIP THE MAYOR OF SWINDON—COUNCILLOR G. H. STEVENS.

PRICES OF ADMISSION :

MATINEES.		EVENINGS.		SATS. & HOLIDAYS.	
Front Stalls ..	6d.	Front Stalls ..	6d.	Front Stalls ..	6d.
Child	3d.	Centre Stalls ..	1/-	Stalls	1/-
Back Stalls ..	1/-	Back Stalls ..	1/6	Centre Stalls ..	1/6
Child	6d.			Back Stalls ..	2/-

The programme cover from the official opening of the Regent Cinema, Regent Circus, on Monday 16 September 1929. It was opened by Cllr G.H. Stevens, Mayor of Swindon and the first week's film was *Bulldog Drummond*, starring Ronald Colman; this film was advertised as his first 100 per cent talking picture. The cinema manager was A.G. Harman, who had previously been manager of the Palace Theatre, Gorse Hill.

The open air Picture Gardens, *c.* 1908. This was thought to be one of the first, if not the first, cinema in Swindon, and was believed to have been at Regent Circus; judging by the number of seats there was room for several hundred people per performance.

The Palladium Cinema under construction in Jennings Street, Rodbourne, 1925. One of several local cinemas opened in Swindon in the 1920s, it finally closed its doors in the late 1950s. The building is now used by Timeprint.

SAVOY CINEMA, SWINDON, BY NIGHT.

A night view of the Savoy Cinema, Regent Street, 1937. The cinema was opened in January 1937, with seating for 1,775 people. (See also *Swindon in Old Photographs IV*, p. 135.)

Swindon GWR Male Voice Choir after winning the Lydney Musical Festival, 1 July 1930. Amongst those identified in the back row are Dick Hobbs, Stan Richens, ? Howell, George Hughes; in the second row are Bert Owen, Francis Crane, Archie Chivers; in the third row are Bert Craddock, Reg Jones, Reg Legg, Reg Cottrell, Ralph Patton; in the front row are ? Webb, Harry Robinson, Alan Moncrieff, Frank Swift, Ethel Barnett (pianist), George Morse (conductor), Bert Billet, ? Holloway, Billy Richardson. Bert Billet and Mr Holloway were both engine drivers and had been members of the choir since its formation. Francis Crane subsequently became conductor during the 1950s. Billy Richardson (second from right in the front row), in addition to being a member of the choir, was also a well-known local entertainer and broadcaster in the 1920s and 1930s. He lived in Lincoln Street and was a clerk in the GWR Works. He also released a number of records in local dialect, the best known of which was probably *Wot's Ther Price O'Swedes*, for the Swindon Victoria Hospital Carnival Week in June 1930. His granddaughter is the well known television and film actress, Miranda Richardson. The choir was formed in 1919, under the baton of W.J. Evans. In more recent times it changed its title to the Swindon Male Voice Choir and it now attracts members from all walks of life, performing regularly not only in Swindon but all over south and central England and Wales. It celebrated its 75th anniversary in 1994.

Mr W.D. James and his Orchestra outside the Eagle Hotel in Regent Street, 1899. Back row, left to right: Vic Dodson, Mr Hallewell, -?-, Bill Drake, T. Hook, Perce Brett, Mr Ealey. Front row: Mr Gilcrist, Mr Cook, W.D. James, Fred Stone, -?-. Wilfred James came to Swindon in the 1860s as a young child, when his father gained employment as a fitter in the GWR, and later became a clerical officer. Wilfred's and his three brothers' musical talents were encouraged by their uncle, William Hawkins, who was bandmaster of the Wiltshire Volunteer Regiment. The Orchestra played at dances and other musical events in Swindon and district, and travelled as far afield as London. W.D. James was also at various times choirmaster at Christ Church, St Mark's and St Paul's. Of his three brothers (a fourth brother was killed at Rodbourne Lane level-crossing, aged eight, in 1883), Edwin Frederick became a leading bassoon player of the period, was a founder member of the London Symphony Orchestra and later became its chairman.

Harry Smith and his Band, 1935. Front row, left to right: Johnnie Stiles, Norman Cripps, Harry Smith, Roger Summerfield (still at school at the time), Syd Pymm. At the back are Ivor Jefferies and Bert Amor. They are wearing their summer costumes here; in the winter they wore a more traditional outfit.

Alma Jones (later Mrs Tomlinson) playing the accordion. She was a player in the Nom-de-Plume Band that had won the Mayor's Cup in the Town Gardens, in about 1942. Later she joined the Garrards Concert Band, which toured the country playing for the troops during the Second World War.

The New Ambassadors Dance Band, early 1930s. At this time, dance bands were not allowed to perform on Sundays, so they also called themselves The Central Light Orchestra for Sunday only performances (they actually practised in the Central Club). Left to right: Maurice Cole, Ernie Lax, Freddie Dunmore, -?-, Hector Walton; Eddie Whatley is on the drums.

The New Sylvians Dance Band, runners-up in the West of England Dance Band Contest in February 1934. Left to right: Ron Richards, Jim Walker, Ewart Selby, Bert Cullingford, Ken Exton, Curley Vowles, Laurie Westcombe.

The shelf behind the bar at the Kings Head, 52 Fleet Street, 1949. This was known as the musicians' pub. Amongst the trophies can be seen the ultimate for any dance band, the All–Britain Title, won by the Johnnie Stiles Band in 1948. There are also awards to Johnny Moss and his Orchestra and also Jack Baxter.

Johnnie Stiles and his Band after winning the 1948 All–Britain Final of the Dance Band Championship, sponsored by the *Melody Maker*, at Belle Vue, Manchester. Left to right: Harry Smith, Trevor Bennett, Roger Summerfield, Johnnie Stiles, Phil Hillier, Bart Hathaway, Percy Harewood, Gordon Talbot, Frank Clarke, -?-, Ronnie Grant, Jock Walker, John Brett.

Arthur Carron and his concert party, Marlborough Town Hall, October 1948. Left to right: Hubert Tucker, Joyce Sutton, Iris Rainger, Beryldene Hunt, Mrs Duck (Mayoress of Marlborough), Arthur Carron, Ald. J. Duck (Mayor of Marlborough), Nellie Stanton, Marilyn Moreman, W.O. Bullock (compère), Ethel Barnett, Tom Williams. Arthur Carron (formerly Arthur Cox), was born in Swindon and was an internationally famous tenor who launched his professional career with the Old Vic Company in London. Later he was associated with the Sadler's Wells Company and made guest appearances at Covent Garden. He also sang at numerous music festivals in England under the batons of such distinguished conductors as Sir Thomas Beecham, Albert Coates, Sir Henry Wood and Sir John Barbirolli. Carron went to America in 1935 in order to do some special operatic coaching, but an audition at the Metropolitan Opera brought him a contract. He made his Metropolitan début as Canio in *Pagliacci* in December 1936, receiving fifteen curtain calls. He remained with the Metropolitan Opera until 1946 when he returned to England. He then continued to appear at Covent Garden, but also toured the towns and villages of the West Country, with supporting artistes, giving a series of local concerts. He also gave singing lessons from his home in Westlecot Road. Many of the others included in this photograph achieved local distinction for their contribution to music over the years; these included Joyce Cameron (née Sutton) of the Cameron Singers. Tom Williams is shown in *Swindon in Old Photographs IV*, p. 110. Ethel Barnett was also pianist to the Swindon GWR Male Voice Choir (see p. 117).

Section Nine

THROUGH THE LENS OF
ALBERT BEANEY

Albert Beaney outside 50 Beatrice Street, c. 1935.
When he lost his job in the GWR in 1937, the
front bay window pictured behind him became his
'shop window', where he showed a range of the
photographs that he had taken of local children.

These boys are totally engrossed in building their own bogie, using any old pieces of wood and bits from a perambulator. They are in the 'backs' at Beatrice Street, with the timber fence of the railway behind them, in the 1930s.

Children pose in Avening Street, Gorse Hill, 1940s. In the distance can be seen the Gorse Hill Junior School buildings.

The 11th Swindon (All Saints) Wolf Cubs, 1939–40. Amongst those identified in the back row are Dennis Gunning, Denis Robins, Roy Gurney, Ken Henry, David Drew, Norman Rouse, John Stratton; middle row: Cyril Bond, ? Wheeler, David Brown, Gordon Staples, Trevor Bodman, Peter Turner, John Skull; front row: Mervyn Kemp, John Dean, Keith Garside, Eric Comley, David Owen, Maurice Palfrey, ? Bennett, Douglas Martin, Philip Hunt. The houses in the background are in Southbrook Street. John Skull later became a well-known footballer and athlete, playing football for the England Youth Team, Wolverhampton Wanderers and Swindon Town (from 1957 to 1959).

The 19th Swindon (St John's) Boy Scouts, 1939. Amongst those identified in the back row are Ron Bridgeman, Stan Bridgeman, John Little, Larry Sankey, Cyril Price, Hubert Leonard, Eric Day, Ken Cliffe; front row: Eric Bridgeman and John Uren. St John's Church in Aylesbury Street was a daughter church of St Mark's. It was closed in 1956 and demolished shortly afterwards. The vestry of the church is visible on the right. On the left is the Sunday School hall which still stands today and is used by Motolec Ltd as their service centre and workshop area.

Children posing for their picture in Hawkins Street, Rodbourne, 1940s.

The ARP post at the County Ground, 1940. Note the cryptic sign 'Hell's Kitchen'.

These soldiers (believed to be from the Warwickshire Regiment) were stationed in Swindon in 1940. They are shown 'arresting' a local man posing as Adolf Hitler. The photograph was taken at the back of the houses in Chester Street.

Auxiliary Fire Service members outside their sandbagged protected area, *c.* 1940.

Local ARP Wardens in front of their shelter, *c.* 1941. During the Second World War 859 men and women were appointed as wardens in Swindon. Their duties involved responding to air raids in their area, enforcing the blackout, keeping up records of people, and cleaning and issuing respirators.

Auxiliary Fire Service men, posing proudly outside Sub-Station A (the Cromwell Street section), *c.* 1940. The lorry which pulled the pump belonged to Leese Ing's, the Swindon mineral water suppliers.

ARP men with a display of suitable shelters for use by households (or in this case ARP personnel), *c.* 1942. The shelter had been made by E. Hill & Sons, and was officially approved.

Young girls pictured in their costumes before taking part in a Swindon carnival parade. The girls worked in the Nicholson's Raincoat Factory in County Road, and are holding their collecting tins.

Children in Wiltshire Avenue, *c.* 1946. The home-made handcart was used by the children to collect wood from the GWR wood wharf in Whitehouse Road, which they sold around the local houses for pocket money. Back row, left to right: Syd Collins, -?-, Keith Hallard, Derek Hazell. Sitting on the cart is Alan Hazell, and at the front are Reg Collins and Tony Hazell.

Children in the Railway Village, early 1940s. This photograph was taken in Oxford Street, looking towards East Street.

Section Ten

WAR TO VICTORY

VE Party in Westcott Place, May 1945. Mrs Macpherson, the Mayoress (on the left), was presented with a bouquet of flowers by 86-year-old Mrs M.M. Dashfield during the celebrations. In those days of strict rationing, it must have required a major effort by the adults to produce the food for the children to eat.

The Hills Civil Defence Group, c. 1941. The only person so far identified is M. Hills, who is fourth from the left in the front row. The photographer was L. Maylott, whose premises were in Faringdon Street.

Members of the Hills Civil Defence Unit, again pictured at the tennis courts, proudly showing off a new gun. Amongst those so far identified are Wally Cripps, Wally Sharp and Mr Watkins.

The entrance gate to Messrs Short Bros Ltd of Rochester (24 Shop C & W Works), March 1941. During the Second World War, Short Bros used several sites around Swindon, including 24 Shop, which was used for the production of Spitfire aircraft. Spare parts for Hurricane fighters were also made here. Other sites were at Sevenhampton, Stratton St Margaret and South Marston airfield, where Stirling bombers were assembled. For many years after the war this slope was known as 'Shorts Hill' by the locals, before becoming part of the North Star roundabout complex. Clares Equipment Ltd is the current occupant of 24 Shop, producing supermarket display stands and trolleys.

Supervisors and chargehands at Short Bros' Blunsdon Factory, during the Second World War. (See also *Swindon in Old Photographs III*, p. 156.)

Sergeant R.E.A. Potter of the Home Guard, showing the Birley Challenge Cup to colleagues at the postal sorting office. He won the trophy in the individual rifle shooting contest organized by the 5th Battalion, Wiltshire Home Guard, in about 1943. The trophy had been presented to him by Mrs Birley, the widow of the late Colonel Birley, who had originally donated the cup. Sergeant Potter worked as a Swindon postman.

Johnnie Stiles and his band at Coate Water, taking part in a 'Holidays at Home' event during the Second World War. These events were put on for the workers, to give them a much-needed break from the long hours they had to work for the war effort. Among the players are Roger Summerfield, Dennis Shakespeare, Gordon Talbot, Phil Hillier, John ('Jock') Walker, Arthur Marsh, Eric Goodman, Les Taylor and Stiles himself. Alfie Holmes (back row, extreme right) supplied the speakers for the event.

The Band of the 13th Battalion, Wiltshire Home Guard, leading the parade along Wood Street, Old Town, c. 1943. Note that Boot's shopfront is still in the same position.

The 13th Battalion (GWR), Wiltshire Home Guard, held a shooting competition at Liddington on 17 September 1944. The prizes are about to be presented by Mr F.W. Hawksworth JP, Chief Mechanical Engineer of the Great Western Railway.

F1 Shop (blacksmiths) at the GWR works, 2 May 1942. During the war many women were employed doing heavy manual work; Phyllis Bezer, aged twenty, worked here with blacksmith Mr Davis and striker George Hutchings. Notice the chalked V for Victory sign on the side of the cylinder.

Ald. Frederick A. Drinkwater, Mayor of Swindon, inspecting members of the Women's Junior Air Corps at the rear of the Town Hall, 1944. The women trained one night a week at Sanford Street School, practising marching, morse code work, flag signalling and first aid. First aid training also took place in an attic room at Mrs Praeter's house in Victoria Hill, with additional instruction from the local doctor.

The Home Guard Standing Down Parade, in Faringdon Road, 8 November 1944. The salute was taking place outside the GWR swimming baths.

VE celebrations in Farnsby Street, May 1945. The Johnnie Stiles Band provided the music for the dancing.

VE party, Florence Street, May 1945. Tables were set out in the road and seventy children enjoyed themselves eating liberal helpings of ice-cream. After a visit from Alderman and Mrs C.S. Macpherson (Mayor and Mayoress of Swindon), there was dancing, games and pony rides provided by Mr J. Patey. When darkness fell Hitler's effigy was burned on a bonfire.

VE Day, Prospect Hill, May 1945. Among the adults are Mrs ('Grannie') Smith, Olive Heavens, Mrs Lay, May Chequer (holding the baby), Tom Storey, Mrs 'Maggie' Robson, Mrs Wetherall, Mrs Storey, Mrs Skane and Elsie Storey. The children include Brian Smith, Gordon Tuck, Christine Jones, Sylvia Webb, Pat Haines, Doreen Morse, John Haines, Ken Jeans, Desmond Jeans, Alan Jeans (making the V sign), Ken Robson, Jimmy Robson, Pam Robson, Jean Morse, Joyce Haines, Ted Perry, Geoff Heavens, Mervyn Jeans, Brian Morse, Ray Morse, Alan Maggs and Alec Tucker. The landlord of the Beehive public house wheeled a piano out on to the street for a sing-song with the residents during the festivities.

VE party in Brunel Street, May 1945. To the right is Alderman Charles S. Macpherson (Mayor of Swindon); Mrs Phyllis Macpherson (the Mayoress) is cutting the cake.

Returned prisoners of war being entertained by the Mayor of Swindon (Alderman C.S. Macpherson) in the Mayor's Parlour at the Civic Offices, May 1945.

Mr Sheppard, a local haulier, giving rides to the local children on his cart during the VJ celebrations in August 1945. The houses in the background are 589 and 591 Cricklade Road.

The back gardens of houses in Cricklade Road. The party, for all the local residents, was held to celebrate VJ Day, August 1945.

VJ Day party, Bessemer Road, 18 August 1945. Steel Morrison bomb-shelters are being used as tables. These were originally fitted with square mesh netting on the sides, which was used extensively in the gardens around the town after the war, before it finally rusted away.

THE CHANGING
FACE OF SWINDON

*Upper Walcot Farm, c. 1950. The Walcot and Park North housing estates built in the
1950s now completely cover this area, but one of the stone buildings survives and can still
be seen today north of Dulverton Avenue. Lower Walcot Farm, to the west, was also
engulfed by the new development but its farmhouse has survived to this day in
Shrewsbury Road.*

Looking into John Street, 1957. Early in the street's history, there was a bridge connecting John Street with Weymouth Street over the North Wilts. Canal. One of Swindon's early bicycle manufacturers, the Lion Cycle Works, was based in the street.

Plymouth Street, looking east towards Drove Road, April 1966, when there was no difficulty finding a parking space!

Commercial Road, October 1971. Leading the procession are the Swindon Town Girls, a group of majorettes and cheer leaders, who had originally formed during the successful season of 1969. On the left is Harry Lunn's fish bar (he was a former Swindon Town football player). Following the girls is Father Christmas (on a 1938 Dennis fire-engine), on his way to the Bon Marché store.

Commercial Road, looking west towards the Market, April 1966. The old market was closed in 1977 and demolished. The area was used as a car park for many years but, as part of the redevelopment of the town centre, a new market was built on the site; it opened in November 1994.

The junction of Clarence Street and Victoria Road, looking towards the College, April 1966. Barkham's electrical store, on the corner of Byron Street, is now a pizza restaurant.

One of Swindon's easily forgotten streets, Horsell Street, April 1966. This view is looking east towards the first extension of the College, opened in 1961 by the Duke of Edinburgh. These terraced houses were soon to be demolished for the next College extension and car park.

Looking across the car park to the College extension, Regent Circus, 1961. A further extension to the complex was built in 1970, the car park being enlarged at the same time, with Rolleston Street and Horsell Street disappearing for ever.

The Gaumont Cinema, Regent Circus, 1962. Just past the cinema is the Bristol bus stop, and further in the distance is the first extension to the college with Rolleston Street to the right.

The Town Hall and Central Library, Regent Circus, 25 April 1966. The 'temporary' library behind the Town Hall was opened in March 1949 – new premises are still awaited in 1995.

Regent Circus, looking towards the Odeon Cinema (formerly known both as the Regent and the Gaumont), in April 1966. The area around the cenotaph is now a pedestrian walkway.

Regent Circus, looking towards David Greig's grocery shop, 25 April 1966. This building is now occupied by the Co-operative Bank plc. The queue outside Bishop and Edgington's on the left is waiting for the Rodbourne Arms bus to arrive.

Brunel Street, looking north-west towards Cromwell Street, January 1970. Note Norman's furniture and carpet store in Cromwell Street; it later moved to the Brunel Plaza. (See also p. 48.)

Princes Street, looking towards Whale Bridge, 1 May 1965. Some of the houses in the block have already been demolished ready for redevelopment. The shop on the left was the 'Baccy Box' which sold newspapers and cigarettes.

Looking along Gordon Road towards Walker Jackson's garage in Princes Street, 18 March 1964. The advertisement on the end of the building on the right is for Jobs builders suppliers, whose shop was on the corner. The Whale Bridge roundabout is now on the left.

Princess Margaret Hospital, Okus Road, *c.* 1968. Work began on this large new general hospital (800 beds), on a 20 acre site at Okus, in 1957. The first hospital to be approved in the country after the Second World War, it was designed by Messrs Powell and Moya. Princess Margaret laid the first stone on 16 April 1957. The first section was in use by 1960, and Princess Margaret returned in April 1966 to officially open the whole complex.

Whale Bridge roundabout under construction, 1 May 1965. This view is looking south towards the Town Hall, with the Walker Jackson premises to the left. It was difficult for pedestrians to reach Princes Street through the building work.

Islington Street, looking south towards the College, 1 May 1965. The newly built Magistrates Court can be seen at the end of the terraced houses on the left. On the corner is the premises of A.E. Smith & Sons, funeral directors.

Looking along Weymouth Street towards Wellington Street, across the junction of Cheltenham Street in the 1960s. All this area is now under the office blocks and bus station complex.

The last remaining buildings in Wellington Street in 1980. Priston's the dentist and the boarded-up Foss's Hotel are shown just before demolition. This area is now part of the bus station/office development. (See also *Swindon in Old Photographs IV*, p. 61.

The Gas Showrooms on the corner of Temple Street and Regent Street, 1960s. On the left is the wall and corner stonework of the Baptist Tabernacle.

Milford Street, with Beale's café on the corner of Cheltenham Street, 1980. Beale's was a well-known local coffee bar that was very popular with the youth of Swindon during the 1950s and '60s. This area, opposite the end of Fleming Way, has been redeveloped with new road schemes and office blocks. Beales Close nearby commemorates the old coffee bar.

This is the view from Edgeware Road, looking down Sanford Street towards the rear of Tesco's, June 1974. At the end of the terraced houses on the right (Sanford Street) is the Congregational Church (see also p. 88).

The corner of Beatrice Street, looking towards the first of the railway bridges, April 1979. The abutments are all that remain of the bridge that was demolished in 1975. This area was redeveloped when Great Western Way was built and the Cockleberry roundabout was constructed.

Acknowledgements

Once again, the Swindon Society would like to thank all those who contributed to the compilation of this book, especially Society members David Bedford and Brian Bridgeman, who put the book together and selected the photographs to be used, and Jean Allen, for her work towards the production of the book. Thanks also to Society members, David Bedford, Denis Bird, Colin Herbert, Malcolm Franklin and Ken Richman for providing many of the photographs.

Especial thanks are also due to Isobel Thompson of Bath Road Museum, Tim Bryan of the Railway Museum, Borough of Thamesdown Museum Service, Albert Beaney, Roger Maisey, F.C.J. Edwards, Roger Summerfield and Mrs Phyllis Macpherson.

Our thanks also go to the staff of Swindon Reference Library (Wiltshire Library and Museum Service), Wiltshire Police and Wiltshire Newspapers for help and assistance. For individual contributions the Society would like to thank:

Mrs J. Allen • Mr M.P. Barnsley • Mr D. Bateman • Mrs M. Beale
Mr A. Beaney • Mrs A.J. Bedford • Mr D. Bedford • Mrs E. Belcher
Mr D. Bird • Mr B. Bridgeman • Mr R. Bridgeman • Mr and Mrs P. Bristow
Mr T. Bryan • Mr R. Burbidge • Mrs J. Cameron • Mrs J. Clark
Mr R. Cook • Mr B. Davis • Mr C. Davis • Mr D. Dean • Mr J.R. Dean
Mr A. Duke • Mr F. Edwards • Mr J. Fox • Mr G. Franklin • Mr M. Franklin
Mr C. Gwyther • Mr A.G. Harvey • Mr F. Haydon • Mr A.P. Hazell
Mr C. Herbert • Mr R. Hudd • Mr A. Hughes • Mrs M. Huntley
Mr E. James • Mr C. Legg • Miss E. Lewis • Mrs J. Little • Mr D. Luker
Mrs J. McLeod • Mrs P. Macpherson • Mr R. Maisey • Mr T. Moran
Mr R. Morse • Mr J. Plaister • Mrs R. New • Mrs M. Philpin • Mrs Y. Plaum
Mr K. Richman • Mr K. Saunders • Mrs P. Saunders • Mr J. Smith
Mr M. Smith • Mrs E. Soul • Mrs M. Spurling • Mr G. Strudwick
Mr R. Summerfield • Mrs A. Tomlinson • Mrs M. Townsend
Mr D. Trueman • Mr G. Tylee • Mr M. Tyler • Miss J. Walker • Mr G. Weare
Mr P.A. Williams • Mr G. Wirdnam • Mr J. Woodward

Some doubts exist regarding the original source of some of the photographs used in this book and the Swindon Society apologizes for any omissions from the acknowledgements shown above. The Society would also welcome any comments or additional information regarding the photographs in this book or in the previous four volumes. Please contact Brian Bridgeman, Publicity Officer, Swindon Society, 69 Sandringham Road, Swindon, Wiltshire SN3 1HT.

BRITAIN IN OLD PHOTOGRAPHS

To order any of these titles please telephone Littlehampton Book Services on 01903 721596

ALDERNEY

Alderney: A Second Selection, *B Bonnard*

BEDFORDSHIRE

Bedfordshire at Work, *N Lutt*

BERKSHIRE

Maidenhead, *M Hayles & D Hedges*
Around Maidenhead, *M Hayles & B Hedges*
Reading, *P Southerton*
Reading: A Second Selection, *P Southerton*
Sandhurst and Crowthorne, *K Dancy*
Around Slough, *J Hunter & K Hunter*
Around Thatcham, *P Allen*
Around Windsor, *B Hedges*

BUCKINGHAMSHIRE

Buckingham and District, *R Cook*
High Wycombe, *R Goodearl*
Around Stony Stratford, *A Lambert*

CHESHIRE

Cheshire Railways, *M Hitches*
Chester, *S Nichols*

CLWYD

Clwyd Railways, *M Hitches*

CLYDESDALE

Clydesdale, *Lesmahagow Parish Historical Association*

CORNWALL

Cornish Coast, *T Bowden*
Falmouth, *P Gilson*
Lower Fal, *P Gilson*
Around Padstow, *M McCarthy*
Around Penzance, *J Holmes*
Penzance and Newlyn, *J Holmes*
Around Truro, *A Lyne*
Upper Fal, *P Gilson*

CUMBERLAND

Cockermouth and District, *J Bernard Bradbury*
Keswick and the Central Lakes, *J Marsh*
Around Penrith, *F Boyd*
Around Whitehaven, *H Fancy*

DERBYSHIRE

Derby, *D Buxton*
Around Matlock, *D Barton*

DEVON

Colyton and Seaton, *T Gosling*
Dawlish and Teignmouth, *G Gosling*
Devon Aerodromes, *K Saunders*
Exeter, *P Thomas*
Exmouth and Budleigh Salterton, *T Gosling*
From Haldon to Mid-Dartmoor, *T Hall*
Honiton and the Otter Valley, *J Yallop*
Around Kingsbridge, *K Tanner*
Around Seaton and Sidmouth, *T Gosling*
Seaton, Axminster and Lyme Regis, *T Gosling*

DORSET

Around Blandford Forum, *B Cox*
Bournemouth, *M Colman*
Bridport and the Bride Valley, *J Burrell & S Humphries*
Dorchester, *T Gosling*
Around Gillingham, *P Crocker*

DURHAM

Darlington, *G Flynn*
Darlington: A Second Selection, *G Flynn*
Durham People, *M Richardson*
Houghton-le-Spring and Hetton-le-Hole, *K Richardson*
Houghton-le-Spring and Hetton-le-Hole:
  A Second Selection, *K Richardson*
Sunderland, *S Miller & B Bell*
Teesdale, *D Coggins*
Teesdale: A Second Selection, *P Raine*
Weardale, *J Crosby*
Weardale: A Second Selection, *J Crosby*

DYFED

Aberystwyth and North Ceredigion,
  Dyfed Cultural Services Dept
Haverfordwest, *Dyfed Cultural Services Dept*
Upper Tywi Valley, *Dyfed Cultural Services Dept*

ESSEX

Around Grays, *B Evans*

GLOUCESTERSHIRE

Along the Avon from Stratford to Tewkesbury, *J Jeremiah*
Cheltenham: A Second Selection, *R Whiting*
Cheltenham at War, *P Gill*
Cirencester, *J Welsford*
Around Cirencester, *E Cuss & P Griffiths*
Forest, The, *D Mullin*
Gloucester, *J Voyce*
Around Gloucester, *A Sutton*
Gloucester: From the Walwin Collection, *J Voyce*
North Cotswolds, *D Viner*
Severn Vale, *A Sutton*
Stonehouse to Painswick, *A Sutton*
Stroud and the Five Valleys, *S Gardiner & L Padin*
Stroud and the Five Valleys: A Second Selection,
  S Gardiner & L Padin
Stroud's Golden Valley, *S Gardiner & L Padin*
Stroudwater and Thames & Severn Canals,
  E Cuss & S Gardiner
Stroudwater and Thames & Severn Canals: A Second
  Selection, *E Cuss & S Gardiner*
Tewkesbury and the Vale of Gloucester, *C Hilton*
Thornbury to Berkeley, *J Hudson*
Uley, Dursley and Cam, *A Sutton*
Wotton-under-Edge to Chipping Sodbury, *A Sutton*

GWYNEDD

Anglesey, *M Hitches*
Gwynedd Railways, *M Hitches*
Around Llandudno, *M Hitches*
Vale of Conwy, *M Hitches*

HAMPSHIRE

Gosport, *J Sadden*
Portsmouth, *P Rogers & D Francis*

HEREFORDSHIRE

Herefordshire, *A Sandford*

HERTFORDSHIRE

Barnet, *I Norrie*
Hitchin, *A Fleck*
St Albans, *S Mullins*
Stevenage, *M Appleton*

ISLE OF MAN

The Tourist Trophy, *B Snelling*

ISLE OF WIGHT

Newport, *D Parr*
Around Ryde, *D Parr*

JERSEY

Jersey: A Third Selection, *R Lemprière*

KENT

Bexley, *M Scott*
Broadstairs and St Peter's, *J Whyman*
Bromley, Keston and Hayes, *M Scott*
Canterbury: A Second Selection, *D Butler*
Chatham and Gillingham, *P MacDougall*
Chatham Dockyard, *P MacDougall*
Deal, *J Broady*
Early Broadstairs and St Peter's, *B Wootton*
East Kent at War, *D Collyer*
Eltham, *J Kennett*
Folkestone: A Second Selection, *A Taylor & E Rooney*
Goudhurst to Tenterden, *A Guilmant*
Gravesend, *R Hiscock*
Around Gravesham, *R Hiscock & D Grierson*
Herne Bay, *J Hawkins*
Lympne Airport, *D Collyer*
Maidstone, *I Hales*
Margate, *R Clements*
RAF Hawkinge, *R Humphreys*
RAF Manston, *RAF Manston History Club*
RAF Manston: A Second Selection,
  RAF Manston History Club
Ramsgate and Thanet Life, *D Perkins*
Romney Marsh, *E Carpenter*
Sandwich, *C Wanostrocht*
Around Tonbridge, *C Bell*
Tunbridge Wells, *M Rowlands & I Beavis*
Tunbridge Wells: A Second Selection,
  M Rowlands & I Beavis
Around Whitstable, *C Court*
Wingham, Adisham and Littlebourne, *M Crane*

LANCASHIRE

Around Barrow-in-Furness, *J Garbutt & J Marsh*
Blackpool, *C Rothwell*
Bury, *J Hudson*
Chorley and District, *J Smith*
Fleetwood, *C Rothwell*
Heywood, *J Hudson*
Around Kirkham, *C Rothwell*
Lancashire North of the Sands, *J Garbutt & J Marsh*
Around Lancaster, *S Ashworth*
Lytham St Anne's, *C Rothwell*
North Fylde, *C Rothwell*
Radcliffe, *J Hudson*
Rossendale, *B Moore & N Dunnachie*

LEICESTERSHIRE

Around Ashby-de-la-Zouch, *K Hillier*
Charnwood Forest, *I Keil, W Humphrey & D Wix*
Leicester, *D Burton*
Leicester: A Second Selection, *D Burton*
Melton Mowbray, *T Hickman*
Around Melton Mowbray, *T Hickman*
River Soar, *D Wix, P Shacklock & I Keil*
Rutland, *T Clough*
Vale of Belvoir, *T Hickman*
Around the Welland Valley, *S Mastoris*

LINCOLNSHIRE

Grimsby, *J Tierney*
Around Grimsby, *J Tierney*
Grimsby Docks, *J Tierney*
Lincoln, *D Cuppleditch*

Scunthorpe, *D Taylor*
Skegness, *W Kime*
Around Skegness, *W Kime*

LONDON

Balham and Tooting, *P Loobey*
Crystal Palace, Penge & Anerley, *M Scott*
Greenwich and Woolwich, *K Clark*
Hackney: A Second Selection, *D Mander*
Lewisham and Deptford, *J Coulter*
Lewisham and Deptford: A Second Selection, *J Coulter*
Streatham, *P Loobey*
Around Whetstone and North Finchley, *J Heathfield*
Woolwich, *B Evans*

MONMOUTHSHIRE

Chepstow and the River Wye, *A Rainsbury*
Monmouth and the River Wye, *Monmouth Museum*

NORFOLK

Great Yarmouth, *M Teun*
Norwich, *M Colman*
Wymondham and Attleborough, *P Yaxley*

NORTHAMPTONSHIRE

Around Stony Stratford, *A Lambert*

NOTTINGHAMSHIRE

Arnold and Bestwood, *M Spick*
Arnold and Bestwood: A Second Selection, *M Spick*
Changing Face of Nottingham, *G Oldfield*
Mansfield, *Old Mansfield Society*
Around Newark, *T Warner*
Nottingham: 1944–1974, *D Whitworth*
Sherwood Forest, *D Ottewell*
Victorian Nottingham, *M Payne*

OXFORDSHIRE

Around Abingdon, *P Horn*
Banburyshire, *M Barnett & S Gosling*
Burford, *A Jewell*
Around Didcot and the Hagbournes, *B Lingham*
Garsington, *M Gunther*
Around Henley-on-Thames, *S Ellis*
Oxford: The University, *J Rhodes*
Thame to Watlington, *N Hood*
Around Wallingford, *D Beasley*
Witney, *T Worley*
Around Witney, *C Mitchell*
Witney District, *T Worley*
Around Woodstock, *J Bond*

POWYS

Brecon, *Brecknock Museum*
Welshpool, *E Bredsdorff*

SHROPSHIRE

Shrewsbury, *D Trumper*
Whitchurch to Market Drayton, *M Morris*

SOMERSET

Bath, *J Hudson*
Bridgwater and the River Parrett, *R Fitzhugh*
Bristol, *D Moorcroft & N Campbell-Sharp*
Changing Face of Keynsham,
    B Lowe & M Whitehead

Chard and Ilminster, *G Gosling & F Huddy*
Crewkerne and the Ham Stone Villages,
    G Gosling & F Huddy
Around Keynsham and Saltford, *B Lowe & T Brown*
Midsomer Norton and Radstock, *C Howell*
Somerton, Ilchester and Langport, *G Gosling & F Huddy*
Taunton, *N Chipchase*
Around Taunton, *N Chipchase*
Wells, *C Howell*
Weston-Super-Mare, *S Poole*
Around Weston-Super-Mare, *S Poole*
West Somerset Villages, *K Houghton & L Thomas*

STAFFORDSHIRE

Aldridge, *J Farrow*
Bilston, *E Rees*
Black Country Transport: Aviation, *A Brew*
Around Burton upon Trent, *G Sowerby & R Farman*
Bushbury, *A Chatwin, M Mills & E Rees*
Around Cannock, *M Mills & S Belcher*
Around Leek, *R Poole*
Lichfield, *H Clayton & K Simmons*
Around Pattingham and Wombourne, *M Griffiths,*
    P Leigh & M Mills
Around Rugeley, *T Randall & J Anslow*
Smethwick, *J Maddison*
Stafford, *J Anslow & T Randall*
Around Stafford, *J Anslow & T Randall*
Stoke-on-Trent, *I Lawley*
Around Tamworth, *R Sulima*
Around Tettenhall and Codsall, *M Mills*
Tipton, Wednesbury and Darlaston, *R Pearson*
Walsall, *D Gilbert & M Lewis*
Wednesbury, *I Bott*
West Bromwich, *R Pearson*

SUFFOLK

Ipswich: A Second Selection, *D Kindred*
Around Ipswich, *D Kindred*
Around Mildenhall, *C Dring*
Southwold to Aldeburgh, *H Phelps*
Around Woodbridge, *H Phelps*

SURREY

Cheam and Belmont, *P Berry*
Croydon, *S Bligh*
Dorking and District, *K Harding*
Around Dorking, *A Jackson*
Around Epsom, *P Berry*
Farnham: A Second Selection, *J Parratt*
Around Haslemere and Hindhead, *T Winter & G Collyer*
Richmond, *Richmond Local History Society*
Sutton, *P Berry*

SUSSEX

Arundel and the Arun Valley, *J Godfrey*
Bishopstone and Seaford, *P Pople & P Berry*
Brighton and Hove, *J Middleton*
Brighton and Hove: A Second Selection, *J Middleton*
Around Crawley, *M Goldsmith*
Hastings, *P Haines*
Hastings: A Second Selection, *P Haines*
Around Haywards Heath, *J Middleton*
Around Heathfield, *A Gillet & B Russell*
Around Heathfield: A Second Selection,
    A Gillet & B Russell
High Weald, *B Harwood*
High Weald: A Second Selection, *B Harwood*
Horsham and District, *T Wales*

Lewes, *J Middleton*
RAF Tangmere, *A Saunders*
Around Rye, *A Dickinson*
Around Worthing, *S White*

WARWICKSHIRE

Along the Avon from Stratford to Tewkesbury, *J Jeremiah*
Bedworth, *J Burton*
Coventry, *D McGrory*
Around Coventry, *D McGrory*
Nuneaton, *S Clews & S Vaughan*
Around Royal Leamington Spa, *J Cameron*
Around Royal Leamington Spa: A Second Selection,
    J Cameron
Around Warwick, *R Booth*

WESTMORLAND

Eden Valley, *J Marsh*
Kendal, *M & P Duff*
South Westmorland Villages, *J Marsh*
Westmorland Lakes, *J Marsh*

WILTSHIRE

Around Amesbury, *P Daniels*
Chippenham and Lacock, *A Wilson & M Wilson*
Around Corsham and Box, *A Wilson & M Wilson*
Around Devizes, *D Buxton*
Around Highworth, *G Tanner*
Around Highworth and Faringdon, *G Tanner*
Around Malmesbury, *A Wilson*
Marlborough: A Second Selection, *P Colman*
Around Melksham,
    Melksham and District Historical Association
Nadder Valley, *R. Sawyer*
Salisbury, *P Saunders*
Salisbury: A Second Selection, *P Daniels*
Salisbury: A Third Selection, *P Daniels*
Around Salisbury, *P Daniels*
Swindon: A Third Selection, *The Swindon Society*
Swindon: A Fourth Selection, *The Swindon Society*
Trowbridge, *M Marshman*
Around Wilton, *P Daniels*
Around Wootton Bassett, Cricklade and Purton, *T Sharp*

WORCESTERSHIRE

Evesham to Bredon, *F Archer*
Around Malvern, *K Smith*
Around Pershore, *M Dowty*
Redditch and the Needle District, *R Saunders*
Redditch: A Second Selection, *R Saunders*
Around Tenbury Wells, *D Green*
Worcester, *M Dowty*
Around Worcester, *R Jones*
Worcester in a Day, *M Dowty*
Worcestershire at Work, *R Jones*

YORKSHIRE

Huddersfield: A Second Selection, *H Wheeler*
Huddersfield: A Third Selection, *H Wheeler*
Leeds Road and Rail, *R Vickers*
Pontefract, *R van Riel*
Scarborough, *D Coggins*
Scarborough's War Years, *R Percy*
Skipton and the Dales, *Friends of the Craven Museum*
Around Skipton-in-Craven, *Friends of the Craven Museum*
Yorkshire Wolds, *I & M Sumner*